# Buying Your First (or Next) Horse:

## 92 Essential Tips to Help You Find Your Dream Horse

**By Anne Gage**

*Author of Confident Rider Confident Horse*

*Disclaimer of Liability*

The author shall have neither liability nor responsibility to any
person or entity with respect to any loss or damage caused or
alleged to be caused directly or indirectly by the information
contained in this book. While the book is as accurate as the
author can make it, there may be errors, omissions or
inaccuracies.

# Table of Contents

## Introduction

Buying a horse is a lot like buying a used car. It's exciting. It's a large financial investment. It requires research, some experienced help and smart buying strategies to make a purchase you'll be happy with. But buying a horse involves an emotional investment on top of the financial one, and the commitment of caring for an animal for many years. So, while the prospect of buying a horse is exciting, it can also be overwhelming.

Unfortunately, some horse sellers – like some used car salesman – have earned a reputation as unscrupulous people who downplay (or disguise) flaws, enhance attributes and only want to get your money. There are many good and reputable people in the horse business who really do care about finding the right match for their horse.

With our emotional connection to these beautiful and sensitive animals it's easy to let our hearts rule our heads. Your buying decision requires careful thought and planning. It's very easy to get caught up in the excitement and emotions of choosing a horse.

I have written this guide with the adult pleasure rider in mind. Whether you intend to ride in an arena, on the trails or participate in schooling level shows, you want to buy a horse that will suit your temperament, riding abilities and riding goals for many years – perhaps even a lifetime. These tips and strategies can help you make smart choices and make your buying experience a good one. Buying the right horse for you is essential for ensuring a happy future for both you and your horse.

# Before You Start Looking

**1. Answer the question "Why do you want to buy a horse?"** Horse ownership is a major commitment of money, time and emotions. If the answer to the question is only about you, what you will get out of it, and not about the horse and what he will get out of it, you (and the horse) may be better off part-boarding or leasing a horse for now.

**2. Create a binder, notebook or file (paper or electronic)** to keep notes, photos and contact information. Take it with you when you start looking at horses. Having this information all in one place will make it easier to keep track of the horses you have seen and make comparisons between them.

*You can download a free **Contact Form** for keeping track of the horses that interest you,  Use the link on  page 4.*

**3. Make a budget** – There are expenses beyond the purchase price when buying a horse. Make sure to plan for retail sales tax, veterinary exam, commissions to an agent (or your coach) and trailering from the seller to the farm where you'll be keeping your horse. Be prepared to have to buy new blankets and tack – even if this is not your first horse.

*You can download a free  Excel spreadsheet to help calculate the costs of buying and keeping a horse .  Use the link on page 4.*

**4.  Be clear on your goals and riding ability**. Focus on what you want to do with your own horse rather than what someone else thinks you should be doing.  Be honest about your skills and abilities with handling as well as riding a horse.  This is not the time for exaggeration.

**5.  Research different breeds.**  Identify the temperament, size, conformation and personality that best suits you, your skills and your riding goals.  A young, flashy Thoroughbred or Arabian might catch your eye, but if your schedule allows you only the occasional trail ride or you can only ride on week-ends, an older, Quarter Horse or draft cross with a calmer temperament will probably suit your needs better.

**6.  Make a list of all the things you want from your ideal horse.**  Keep in mind your budget, horsemanship and riding skill levels, the type of riding you will be doing and how often you will be riding.

**7.  Prepare a check list of questions.**  Before going to see any horses, create a check-list of questions that you want to ask the seller. It's very easy to get caught up in the excitement of shopping and forget the important issues.  Having your list of questions to review at the meeting will ensure you have the answers you need before making a decision.

*You can download a free Horse Buyer's Pre-Visit Questionnaire.  Use the link on page 4*

**8.  If you'll be boarding your horse.** Before you buy your horse, find a facility that provides quality care, is within your budget and will have space available for your horse when you complete your purchase.

**9. If you'll be keeping your horse at home.** Before bringing your <u>horse home</u>, ensure you have set up a safe paddock area with access to water, shelter (a run in and/or barn), hay and feed storage. Horses are social animals and need the company of at least one other horse for their emotional well being.

**10. Find a vet and a farrier.** If you will be boarding, the facility will be able to recommend the professionals they use. If keeping your horse at home, ask your coach or other horse people in the area for recommendations. Contact a vet and farrier to ensure they are taking on new clients.

**11. Hire an Expert as an adviser.** This can be your coach or another experienced horse person. Make sure that your Expert is knowledgeable about horses as well as the discipline you want to ride in. He or she should also be aware of your goals, abilities and riding and horsemanship skills.

**12. Ask up front what fees the Expert charges.** Having a professional opinion from a person with no emotional or financial attachment to your potential purchase is invaluable. So, expect to pay them for their time. Ask up front how much this service will cost and if they also charge a commission on the final purchase. Include these fees in your budget so that there are no surprises.

**13. Sales Commissions.** Much like in real estate transactions, most professionals charge a commission on horse sales they handle for their clients. If 2 professionals are involved, there may be 2 commissions to be paid – one to the seller's agent (paid by the seller) and one to the buyer's trainer (paid by the buyer). Commission rates for buyers can run from 10-20% of the purchase price.

**14. If your Expert does not want to charge you for their help,** offer a token of your appreciation once you have bought your horse. A gift certificate to a tack shop or restaurant, a bottle of wine, or some homemade cookies are good options.

**15. Listen to your Expert's advice.** If your Expert does not approve of the horse, do not buy it. No matter how much you may want it, trust the opinion of the trained professional who is looking out for your best interests.

---

## FREE FILES TO DOWNLOAD

**Contact Form** in PDF format for keeping track of the horses that interest you:

www.confidenthorsemanship.com/wp-content/uploads/ 2015/10/ Contact-Form.pdf

**Cost of Buying and Keeping a Horse** – an Excel spreadsheet:

www.confidenthorsemanship.com/wp-content/uploads/2015/10/Cost-of-Buying-and-Keeping-a -Horse.xlsx

**Horse Buyer's Pre-Visit Questionnaire** – PDF file:
www.confidenthorsemanship.com/wp-content/uploads/2015/10/ Pre-Visit-Questionnaire1.pdf

---

# Where to Look

**16.  Word of mouth.** Let your horse friends and contacts know you are looking to buy a horse.  Many good horses are never advertised.

**17.  Visit online horse classifieds websites.** These sites allow you to narrow your search by location, breed, age, discipline, etc. Many ads include photos or videos.

**18.  Read printed horse trader magazines.** These magazines usually cater to a specific geographical area.  They are printed once a month and are available at tack and feed shops.

**19.  Check local bulletin boards.** Most feed and tack shops have a board where people can post notices for horse related services and horses for sale.  Ask the store staff if they are familiar with the horse or the person who posted the ad.

**20.  Consider adopting from a Horse Rescue.** There is probably a rescue facility in your area. This is not necessarily the best place for  a first time horse owner to look because many horses in rescues have been abused or neglected and may require additional training. Be very honest about your skills, experience and abilities on the adoption application.

**21.  Be careful at livestock auctions.** Usually held monthly, this is the most risky way to purchase a horse and is best left to the very knowledgeable and those willing to return the horse to another auction. Training issues, health problems and lameness can be hidden with drugs.

**22. Registered Auctions**. Less risky than livestock auctions because the owners provide pedigrees, vet information (including x-rays) and prospective buyers can ride the horse. However, it often leads to impulse buying and buyer's remorse shortly after.

**23. Be aware that descriptions given in ads are not always accurate.** If the ad describes the horse as 'good to load, clip, shoe and hacks well', ask to see the horse do all those things. If it's true and you are seriously considering buying the horse, the seller should be willing to show you how the horse behaves under these conditions – even if it means coming back for more than one visit.

**24. Prioritize your list.** Begin your list with horses that meet all of your requirements of age, gender, breed and are within an area that you can comfortably drive to and from in less than a day. You will schedule appointments to meet the seller and the horse in person before buying.

**25. Ask around**. Whether you are buying from an individual, a horse dealer or a trainer, the horse community is small. Ask your horse contacts if they are familiar with the horse, the horse's owner or the person selling the horse and about their reputation.

**26. Look for a horse that 'is'.** A horse that already does rather than one that 'will be' or 'could be' doing what you want to do. If the seller says that the horse has the 'potential to ...' that means you'll have to put time and training into him. It could take years to develop a horse's 'potential'.

**27. Review your list with your coach or experienced person.** Based on their comments, narrow your list to the most appropriate horses to enquire about.

**28. Only consider horses you can go to see and try in person.** Finding a horse is a bit like internet dating – what you see online is not necessarily what you get. If you wouldn't consider marrying someone without at least meeting them a few times (even arranged marriages get supervised 'dates'), why would you commit to an equine partner without doing the same?

# Etiquette When Trying Horses

**29. Contact the seller by phone or email.** Ask your initial questions and decide if you want to take the horse off your list or schedule an appointment to try him. Prepare your questions using the Pre-Visit Questionnaire

**30. Schedule appointments.** Always contact the seller to schedule an appointment. You can save time by scheduling several appointments in the same area on one day.

**31. Get directions from the seller**. Email is the best way to get accurate directions and ask any follow up questions.

**32. Call if you cancel**. If you aren't going to make it to a scheduled appointment or you are going to be more than 15 minutes late, call the seller and let him or her know. His or her time is valuable and they would much rather know you aren't going to show up than to have their horse ready and be waiting.

**33. Leave your entourage at home**. Particularly for the first visit, take one person who can be a voice of reason, a sounding board, take video or photos and keep you calm. This person can be a trusted friend or your Expert. Leave the kids and the dog at home – they'll only be a distraction and take your focus off the horse.

**34. Coach your travelling companion.** Ask anyone accompanying you to see the horse to save their opinions for the ride home. They should avoid mentioning price or your horse-buying budget and not be negative or overly enthusiastic about the horse in front of the seller. (They should also understand that you will not buy any horse until your instructor has approved it.)

**35. Ask for permission before handling the horse.** Some sellers are very cautious about someone they don't know handling their horse. Let them show you the horse first and then ask if you can lead, groom, untack or turn out the horse.

# What to Look For When Trying Horses

**36. Put temperament and training at the top of your priority list.** Papers, colour and appearance don't mean a thing if the he horse's temperament doesn't suit you or he needs a lot of training to do what you need. A well-trained, ugly (if there is such a thing) horse with a good temperament will be a much better partner than the beautiful, registered, green horse with challenging personality traits.

**37. If the horse is registered, ask to see original papers.** The description should fit the horse and the seller should be listed as the current owner.

**38. Note the horse's overall condition.** His ribs should not be visible and he should have good muscle tone rather than flabbiness. His coat should be shiny and healthy looking rather than dull, dry and without bald patches His eyes and nostrils should be clear and clean. His feet should be in good condition – no chips, flares or cracks.

**39. Observe the horse's behaviour** on his own and with other horses while he is being ridden, in the barn and in the paddock. Let the seller know beforehand that you want to see the horse being handled - being lead, tied, groomed, tacked up and turned out.

**40. Ask the seller if the horse has any stable vices.** Weaving, cribbing and stall kicking are all habits that are difficult to deal with. Look for signs of these behaviours (eg. stall doors or paddock fences damaged by chewing; stall walls damaged from kicking)

**41. Notice the horse's responsiveness to his environment.** If the horse's behaviour is very quiet, check that he is paying attention and has some interest in the people and activities around him. Horses who seem very stoic (unresponsive, not blinking, not interacting, appear aloof) may be emotionally shut down or may have been drugged to appear calm.

**42. Notice the horse's reaction when he is touched.** Stroke the horse's neck, back, girth, haunches and legs. Notice if he shows any signs of tension (eg. tight muscles, flinching, tight mouth, pinched nostrils, etc.) or if he feels relaxed and enjoys the attention.

**43. Watch the horse move at liberty.** Ask the seller to turn the horse loose in the paddock or arena and move him around at walk, trot and canter. If you're looking for a jumping partner, ask to see him free jump. How a horse moves without a rider, tells you a lot about their natural movement, rhythm and carriage as well as soundness.

**44. Watch the seller tack up the horse.** The horse should stand quietly and calmly while being saddled, girthed or cinched, and bridled. Signs of unease (i.e. dancing on the cross ties, head tossing, ear pinning, opening mouth or biting) while being groomed or saddled, or resistance to taking the bit can indicate the horse has pain or training issues.

**45. Ask about the type of tack the horse is ridden with.** A well trained, quiet horse should not need more than a well fitting saddle and snaffle bit bridle. If a stronger bit or more equipment is being used, ask the seller 'why' and if you can see the horse ridden without any gadgets (eg. draw reins, tie downs, running martingale, flash nose band, harsh bit, spurs, etc.)

**46. Watch the seller ride the horse before you do.** If they aren't willing to or seem hesitant, it could mean the horse has a training or behavioural problem.

**47. Pay attention to how the seller rides the horse.** Do they seem to be using more force than you ride with (i.e. kicking, spurring or whipping)?  Ask to see the horse go with contact on the reins and on a loose rein in all gaits.

**48. Keep a record of your observations.** To help keep you focused on your buying criteria during the visit,  keep notes about your initial impression, the horses overall condition, his temperament, way of going, etc.  These notes will be valuable in helping you make your final buying decision and may influence your purchase offer to the buyer.

---

Use the **In Person Evaluation form** to record your observations of the horses you try.

Download this free PDF file at: www.confidenthorsemanship.com/wp-content/uploads/2015/10/In-Person-Evaluation1.pdf

---

# Important Body Language

**49. Body Posture has meaning.** A relaxed and comfortable horse shows no tension in the muscles of his back or neck. He holds his poll at or below his withers (slightly above is OK as long as all the other signs indicate relaxation). He stands with front feet square and may relax one hind leg.

**50. The horse's ears and tail are the clearest indicators of how he feels.** These 2 body parts give the most easily read body language signals. Pay attention to both of them when the horse is being groomed, tacked and ridden. Ideally, the horse should be calm, relaxed and comfortable.

**51. Look for ears that move.** A content, comfortable horse's ears move about as he pays attention to his environment. Pinned ears indicate fear or anger which may be caused by pain or even dislike of people.

**52. Look for a quiet, softly curled tail.** A relaxed, comfortable horse has a quiet, softly curled tail. A swishing tail (if not being used to get rid of flies) indicates annoyance or irritation caused by frustration, pain or conflict. A tail that has been 'blocked' will not move at all.

**53. Look for a soft, relaxed mouth and muzzle.** The mouth, nostrils and chin or a calm horse are soft and relaxed. Tight lips, pinched or flared nostrils indicate fear, anxiety or annoyance. When being ridden, an open or very busy mouth shows resistance, often caused by pain.

**54. Breathing should be quiet and regular.** A healthy, fit horse will have a quiet, regular rate of breathing. Heavy breathing (sides heaving and nostrils flared) or an irregular rate can indicate unfitness, stress or an underlying health problem such as allergies or heaves.

**55. Pawing is a sign of frustration or anxiety.** Pawing while tied, being groomed, tacked up or standing still while mounted can indicate the horse is tense or anxious about being ridden, being alone in the barn or something else in the environment.

**56. Respect for personal space.** The horse may push into your space with his head, shoulder, barrel or hips, to find out if you are a leader or a follower. How he reacts when you ask him to move away from you can indicate his nature or how he has been allowed to behave by other people. A passive, respectful horse moves easily away from your push without any resistance. An assertive or poorly trained horse pushes back, swishes his tail or may threaten to bite, strike or kick.

**57. Notice how the horse behaves while being mounted.** Walking away from the mounting block or needing to be held for mounting is a sign of poor training and/or anxiety in the horse. Look for a horse that stands calmly and patiently while being mounted and only walks off when asked to do so by the rider.

**58. It's okay to walk away.** If at any point in the visit you don't think the horse is suitable for you or shows behaviours that make you feel uncomfortable, just politely tell the seller that the horse is not what you are looking for. Reputable sellers understand that their horse will not suit every rider and they will appreciate you not wasting their time.

# Your Turn to Ride

**59. Have your Expert ride the horse first.** They can test the horse's training for any holes or potential problems. You can see how the horse goes with an unfamiliar rider. Trust and listen to your Expert's opinion on whether or not you should ride the horse.

**60. Go for a ride.** The horse should stand quietly while you mount and wait for you to ask him to walk off. If he seems tense, pins his ears, swishes his tail or pulls on the bit he may be uncomfortable due to pain (ie. poor saddle fit, muscle or chiropractic pain).

**61. Take your first ride in a safe area.** Go slowly and take your time. Notice how comfortable and confident you feel and how well the horse responds. Test all the gaits including halt, stand and back up.

**62. If all goes well, ride in an environment similar to where you will ride.** That could be in the arena (indoor and/or outdoor) and on a short trail ride (even just around the farm), with and without other horses. It may mean more than one trip to the farm when trying a prospective horse, but a good seller will not mind you coming back as long as you are seriously considering purchasing the horse. A seller who cares about the horse wants to make sure it is a good match.

**63. Evaluate the horse's responsiveness to your aids.** If the horse is extremely 'dull' (un-responsive) to your aids, he may be either drugged, emotionally shut down or unhappy about his work. If he seems reactive to your aids he may be more nervous and sensitive a may become more difficult to handle over time. Look for a horse that responds easily to your cues but does not get upset by inadvertent movements of your legs or momentary imbalance.

**64. Spend time with the horse**. Take some time to hang out with the horse, grooming, hand grazing, picking up feet and stroking him. Do all the things you would like to be able to do with your own horse and evaluate how he responds and how you feel about being with him.

**65. Ask questions.** If you have any doubt or misgivings about the horse or his behaviour (eg. cribbing, stall walking, weaving, separation anxiety, girthiness, etc.), question the seller. If they can't offer a reasonable explanation, it could indicate a problem.

**66. Take photos and video.** Have your companion or Expert take videos of the horse while you are handling and riding him. It's good to be able to review them later to see how you look on the horse.

**67. Go home and think about it.** It's never a good idea to buy a horse on first sight. Try the horse more than once and ask lots of questions. Look at other horses besides the one you've fallen in love with and make comparisons. Listen to the advice of your coach or other experienced person. Be absolutely sure you've chosen the horse most suitable for you.

**68. Take your time to decide.** Some sellers will use pressure tactics to push you into a decision by telling you that there is another prospective buyer making an offer or coming to see the horse. If someone else does buy the horse before you make up your mind, remind yourself that there are lots of horses on the market and you will find another horse that suits you.

**69. Go back for another visit.** If you are genuinely interested in the horse and think he is a good match for you and your goals, arrange to visit again and spend more time doing things with him yourself. Think of it as a second date where you can both a bit more relaxed.

**70.  Look at more than one horse.** Even if you fall in love with the first horse you try, take a look at least at 2 or 3 more. Your emotions may muddy your logic and cause you to make a decision too quickly. Looking at others gives you a point of comparison and you can always go back to that first horse if he really is the one for you.

**71.  Take your time**. Having a deadline for buying a horse creates a lot of pressure that may cause you to make an unwise decision.

# Making an Offer to Purchase

**72. Expect to negotiate on the asking price.** A lot like buying a used car, how much the seller is willing to negotiate depends upon market conditions (how likely is it that they can sell the horse quickly at full price), how long the horse has been for sale, the seller's personal financial circumstances, and, to a certain degree, how much the seller likes you and thinks you will provide a good home for their horse.

**73. Before you make an offer,** ask your Expert their opinion on a fair price. You may not want to negotiate if you feel the horse is fairly priced. Keep any offer below 20% of the asking price – on a horse priced at $5000 your lowest offer would be $4000.

**74. If the seller won't negotiate on the price,** they may be willing to include something else for free – shipping the horse for you; including his blankets; or giving you some of his tack.

**75. Tack is rarely included in the sale** unless mentioned up front or negotiated during the offer to purchase. In most provinces and states, the seller is legally required to sell the horse with a halter.

**76. Have a vet check done.** Before completing any purchase, have your own vet (or one that does not know the horse) complete a health exam. Tell the vet what you are looking for in a horse and what you plan on doing with him. You and/or your expert should be present when the exam is done.

**77.  Check more than basic health**. Your vet should check general health, vision, dental health, hoof health and soundness. Also ask him or her to draw blood to keep on file for testing in case the horse's health, soundness or temperament changes dramatically after purchase.  For a performance horse, consider having X-rays.

**78.  If the vet sees anything that causes concern**, he or she will want to discuss it with you. Vets do not 'pass' or 'fail' horses.  They simply tell you their observations and possible prognosis of existing conditions. The final buying decision is yours.

**79.  If the seller tries to dissuade you from doing a vet check, be suspicious** – even if they offer to discount the price. It may seem like an extra expense, but it's worth every cent if it saves you years of vet bills or heart break because of an underlying health problem.

**80.  Ask for a trial period.** Some sellers will allow you to take the horse to your farm for a short period of time (usually about 1 week) so you can see how the horse behaves in a new location and have the vet check done.  You will be expected to ensure the horse is well cared for and return him in the same condition should you change your mind about buying.

**81.  Paying a deposit.** Before the horse goes on trial or the vet check is done, the seller will expect you to pay a deposit.  This amount is usually non-refundable if you return the horse unless the vet check discloses an underlying medical condition making the horse unsuitable for your purposes.

**82.  Have the horse insured.**  Make sure you have insurance coverage from the moment the horse leaves the seller's barn – anything can happen before he reaches your farm or while he is there.  If the horse becomes ill or injured while on the trial period, the seller will expect you to pay the full purchase price or receive a compensation pay-out.

# Before Bringing Your Horse Home

**83. Ask for the horse's full medical history.** Ask the seller or barn manager to provide the most current information of your new horse's vaccinations, de-worming, hoof care and any veterinary care.

**84. If vaccinations or de-worming are not up to date,** have them done a few days before moving your horse to his new home. Horses are more susceptible to infectious diseases when under stress.

**85. Confirm your boarding arrangements.** If boarding your horse, talk with the barn manager to arrange your horse's arrival date and time.

**86. Prepare your home farm.** If keeping your horse at home, check the safety of your barn and paddock. Set up a stall (bedding, feed and water buckets) and turn out area (shelter, feed and water) prior to your horse's arrival.

**87. Arrange shipping.** If you don't have your own trailer, ask the seller if he or she is able to ship the horse for you. (You may be able to negotiate this as part of the purchase price of the horse.) Otherwise, ask your Expert or other horse people who they use and would recommend.

**88. Check your first aid kit.** Be prepared in the event your horse suffers an injury in the excitement of settling in.

**89. Check that your tack fits your horse.** Investing in a saddle, bridle and bit that fit your horse properly will keep your horse happy and comfortable. Ill fitting tack can cause pain that results in 'bad' behaviours (like bucking, bolting, rearing). Enlist the help of an expert such as your coach or a certified saddle fitter.

**90. No new partnership is perfect.** There is no 'perfect match' in any kind of relationship or partnership. Your 'dream' horse will throw some challenges your way, but that's all part of the journey of horse ownership. As you work through them, you'll make your partnership stronger and you will both learn and grow.

**91. Put yourself in your horse's shoes.** Your new horse has just been taken away from everything and everyone he knows. He will need time to adjust to his new surroundings, new routine and new friends (horses and human). Help him do that by spending time bonding with him and getting to know each other.

**92. Be patient and understanding as he adjusts to his new life.** Just like us, horses have different tolerances for change. Some adjust in a few days; others may take a few weeks or even months to settle in.

### *Enjoy the journey!*

For more tips and resources to help you build a trusting, respectful and willing partnership with your horse, visit:
www.ConfidentHorsemanship.com

# About The Author

ANNE GAGE is a Clinician, Coach, Trainer, Writer, and certified Professional Coach with over 25 years experience working with horses and their humans. She has certifications from Chris Irwin (Certified Double Gold Trainer) and Daniel Stewart (Certified Ride Right and Pressure Proof Mentor); and, has studied the work of Linda Tellington Jones (TTouch and TTEAM). But her greatest teachers have been the hundreds of horses she has been honoured to work with.

Anne uses her unique experiences and skills to focus on the mental as well as the physical aspects of horsemanship. She helps her clients to develop good, basic fundamentals in both ground work and riding, improve their and their horse's posture when riding, and understand their horse's natural behaviour. In this way, they are able to develop a willing partnership with their horses based on mutual trust, respect and confidence.

Whether you are new to riding and horsemanship, have years of experience, ride for pleasure or competition, Anne Gage offers coaching, training, clinics, workshops and demonstrations that help you and your horse get the most you can out of whatever you do together.

Anne lives with her husband of 34 years, 2 dogs, 4 cats and 9 horses on their farm in Mono, Ontario, Canada.

Find out more at amazon.com/author/annegage or visit Anne's website at www.ConfidentHorsemanship.com

# Other Books By Anne Gage

## Kindle Books

○ Bringing Your New Horse Home: 37 Essential Tips To Help You And Your Horse Start Your Partnership On The Right Foot

○ Confident Horsemanship: Build Your Confidence While Improving Your Partnership with Your Horse

## Paperback Books

Confident Rider Confident Horse: Build Your Confidence and Develop a True Partnership with Your Horse from the Ground to the Saddle

## *I Need Your Help!*

I hope you received value from this book.

I truly want to help people and their horses by providing valuable and useful information that is easy to understand so that you and your new horse get a good start in your partnership.

You can help me do that.

If you received value from this book and bought it online, please share a short, honest review of it on Amazon or Lulu.com. Quality reviews make a difference and help the book reach more people.

Writing a review on either Amazon or Lulu.com is simple and only takes a couple of minutes. Just visit this book's page and click the 'reviews' link just below the book title.

If you have feedback or suggestions to help improve the book, please contact me at anne@confidenthorsemanship.com

Thank you for your support! I truly appreciate it.

Anne Gage

www.ingramcontent.com/pod-product-compliance
Lightning Source LLC
Chambersburg PA
CBHW030314030426
42337CB00012B/702